INTO THE STORM

How to Turn Adversity Into
Your Advantage

Kevin DeShazo

ISBN-13: 9798332170072

Cover design by: Kevin DeShazo
Printed in the United States of America

To my wife, Megan, for the unwavering belief and support. You're the backbone of all of it.
To my boys Gabe, Noah and Asher, you are consistently the why behind the what. The daily strive to be better is because of and for you. Nothing compares to being your Dad.
To the friends, community, clients, supporters, who believed in me and in this project, I continue to be in awe and forever grateful.
To Stephen Ponder, thanks for the inspiration.

CONTENTS

Title Page   1

Copyright   2

Dedication   3

Introduction   7

Chapter 1: The Oncoming Storm   11

Chapter 2: Lessons from the Meadow   18

Chapter 3: Outrunning the Rain   26

Chapter 4: Finding Your Herd   35

Chapter 5: The Rainbow After the Rain   43

Chapter 6: Navigating Life's Storms   52

Chapter 7: The Bison Mentality Program   57

Chapter 8: The Final Game   63

Epilogue: Embracing the Storm   68

ABOUT THE AUTHOR   71

NOTES   73

NOTES   74

NOTES   75

NOTES   76

NOTES   77

NOTES   78
NOTES   79
NOTES   80
NOTES   81
NOTES   82
NOTES   83
NOTES   84

INTRODUCTION

Winds picked up. Clouds built overhead. A storm was brewing. Amidst the backdrop of the storm stand two creatures, about to make a decision: the bison and the cow. As the dark clouds approach, fear sets in for the cow. In response, it runs away from the storm. It believes it can outrun the inevitable. Its ultimate goal? Comfort. The bison, however, turns its sturdy head toward the storm and begins moving into it. It may not love the storm but it does not fear it. It instinctively knows that the quickest way out is through.

This contrast between the bison and the cow is not just a lesson from nature, but a metaphor for how we, as individuals, face the storms of our lives. Adversities, challenges, and setbacks are inevitable. How we choose to confront them – whether we attempt to evade and prolong our agony or confront them head-on – shapes the trajectory of our lives.

In the ensuing chapters, we'll dive into the life of Alex, a high school student with dreams, ambitions, and a world of potential. Alex, like many of us, faces challenges. Some manifest on the sports field, as sweat-soaked jerseys and bruised shins, while others simmer quietly under the surface, in the form of anxiety, self-doubt, and fear of failure. These storms, both external and internal, threaten to throw Alex off course, to drench his dreams and aspirations in torrents of despair.

But storms are not only about rain, wind, and thunder; they're also about resilience, learning, and growth. Enter Alex's father, a beacon of wisdom, who, having navigated his own storms, wishes to impart lessons to his child. He turns to nature, drawing parallels between the bison and the cow to teach Alex – and us – invaluable life lessons.

Lesson 1: You can't avoid the storm. Just as the sun guarantees the day and the moon heralds the night, adversity is a guarantee in life. We cannot run from it, nor can we wish it away. It will come, as surely as the changing seasons.

Lesson 2: Trying to avoid the storm only makes things worse. Much like the cow that tries to outrun the storm and ends up spending more time in the rain, evading challenges only amplifies them. The storm will catch up, and when it does, it finds us exhausted, unprepared, and still drenched. The only way through it is through it.

Lesson 3: There is power in the herd. In isolation, we are vulnerable. But united, with a supportive community around us – be it friends, family, or mentors – we have the collective strength to face any storm.

Lesson 4: Every storm runs out of rain. This too shall pass.

No matter how daunting the adversity, it is but a temporary phase. It is not the whole of our story, just a chapter in it. A season. The skies will clear, and the sun will shine again.

Lesson 5: Do hard things. To truly brace ourselves for life's storms, we must venture out into the rain deliberately, challenge ourselves, and build our resilience. It's in the act of facing adversity that we learn how to triumph over it. This is where your mindset is critical. You will face adversity in life. You will get knocked down. How you think determines how you respond. Mental toughness is not about not getting knocked down. It is about getting back up. Resilience comes from doing hard things.

In the heart of this book is not just the story of a young individual facing life's challenges, but a universal tale of resilience, growth, and triumph. It's about every one of us, our personal storms, and the choices we make. As we delve into Alex's journey, you might see glimpses of your own story, your own challenges, and hopefully, draw inspiration to turn toward your storms, just as the bison does.

Before we embark on this journey, take a deep breath. Imagine that vast meadow with the impending storm, and ask yourself: Are you the cow, choosing the path of fear and resistance, or the bison, embracing the storm with courage and conviction?

Whichever you identify with now, by the end of this tale, we hope you'll have the mentality of the bison, ready to charge into the storm, confident in your strength to not only survive but thrive.

Welcome to the journey. Let's brave the storm together.

CHAPTER 1: THE ONCOMING STORM

The school bell echoed throughout the corridor, signaling the end of the day. Students spilled out of their classrooms, their chatter filling the hallways with the latest gossip, weekend plans, and the ever-present lament over homework. Among the crowd was Alex, his gym bag slung over one shoulder and headphones hanging around his neck. Though he seemed like any other high schooler, with his untied sneakers and untamed hair, there was something that set him apart. On the field, Alex was magic. Soccer was his passion, his escape, and, most importantly, his ticket to a better future. Scouts had started to show up to his games, whispers of college scholarships were in the air, and the weight of expectation rested heavily on his young shoulders.

The sky was a mix of oranges and pinks as he made his way to the soccer field for practice. He exchanged easy banter with teammates, all while going through the motions of stretching and warm-up drills. But today, something felt off. Every time he kicked the ball, a sharp pain shot up his leg. He tried to shake it off, attributing it to fatigue or perhaps a minor strain. But as the practice began and the pace picked up, that nagging pain became increasingly persistent. He knew this pain wasn't normal and considered stepping off the field to go see the trainer, but talked himself out of it. "It's fine," he thought. "It'll go away as practice goes on. I'm good."

In a crucial play, with Alex sprinting towards the goal, he pivoted to dodge an opponent. A wrong step, a twisted ankle, and a world of pain later, he found himself crumpled on the field, clutching his knee, a chorus of gasps surrounding him.

The school's athletic trainer rushed to his side, followed closely by the coach. The initial prognosis wasn't good. Alex was helped off the field, each step a painful reminder of the fragility of dreams. A few days later, the local clinic's fluorescent lights buzzed overhead as the doctor confirmed their worst fears as he looked over the results from the MRI: a torn ACL. Surgery, followed by months of rehabilitation, was inevitable. The season was over for Alex, and with it, the hopes of a scholarship dimmed.

Alex returned home, the weight of disappointment dragging him down. "Why me? Why now? I don't deserve this," he questioned to nobody in particular as he sat alone in his room. He felt trapped, ensnared by circumstances beyond his control. Instead of confronting reality, he sought refuge in denial. "Maybe the doctor was wrong," he thought. "I bet a second opinion would show it's not a big deal. It's just a minor injury." He'd heard stories of athletes bouncing back quickly, and he clung to those narratives, avoiding the storm cloud that loomed ever so large.

After sulking all day, dinner was a somber affair. Alex's

younger sister, Grace, eyed him with concern, her innocent questions about his knee making him wince. His mother tried to infuse the room with optimism, speaking of silver linings and new beginnings. Alex tried to act like nothing was wrong, that everything was fine. "I'm sure the doctors didn't see it clearly. I'll be good in a week," he said with faux confidence. But it was his father, silent throughout dinner, who held Alex's attention.

Once the dishes were cleared, Alex's father motioned for him to join him on the porch. The evening was cool, the onset of autumn noticeable in the rustling leaves and the crisp air. They sat side by side in comfortable silence, the vast expanse of their family's property stretching out in front of them. A storm was brewing in the distance, the dark clouds a mirror of the turmoil in Alex's heart and mind.

"I've seen many storms in my life," his father began, his voice calm and steady. "Some I saw coming, others took me by surprise. But one thing remained consistent – they always passed. Without fail, every storm runs out of rain."

Alex remained silent, his gaze fixed on the horizon.

"I know you're scared, son. And it's okay to be. But running away from our problems, denying their existence, is like that cow in the field, trying to outrun the storm." He pointed towards the far end of their property, where a lone cow was making its way, its pace hurried, its direction away from the impending storm.

Alex frowned, the analogy puzzling him. "I don't get it, Dad. Are you saying I'm a cow?"

His father laughed. "Not exactly. What I'm trying to say is, there's a lesson to be learned from nature. From the bison and the cow."

As the first raindrops began to fall, Alex felt the weight of his father's arm around his shoulders, and the reality of his situation began to sink in. He leaned in, comforted by the warmth, ready to hear the tale of the bison and the cow. Unbeknownst to him, this story was about to change the course of his life.

The storm was approaching, but with it came lessons, wisdom, and a journey of self-discovery. Alex was at the cusp of a transformation, standing at the crossroads between denial and acceptance, between running away and facing adversity head-on. And as the rain lashed down, he realized that the real storm wasn't the one in the sky; it was the one brewing within him.

Reflection Exercise: Facing The Storm Head-On

Objective: To encourage individuals or teams to confront challenges and adversities rather than avoiding them, drawing inspiration from the first lesson of the bison and the cow.

Instructions:

Individual Reflection (10 minutes):

- Begin by asking each participant to close their eyes and recall a time when they faced a challenge or adversity in their lives.

- Ask them to remember how it felt at that moment – the emotions, the fears, the uncertainties.

- Now, have them think about how they approached that challenge. Did they face it head-on like the bison or tried to avoid it like the cow?

Journaling (15 minutes):

- Ask participants to write down the challenge they thought of in their journal.

- Underneath, they should note down their initial reaction to the challenge. Was it avoidance, fear, or confrontation?

- Next, ask them to reflect and jot down what they learned from that experience, and how they might approach a similar challenge in the future.

Group Sharing (If applicable, 20 minutes):

- Invite participants to share their reflections with the group. This is a space for open dialogue, and there should be no judgment.

- As each participant shares, others can provide feedback, offer support, or share similar experiences. The objective is to create a supportive environment and learn from each other.

Group Discussion (15 minutes):

- Delve into a conversation about why we sometimes choose to avoid challenges. Discuss the short-term and long-term effects of avoidance.

- Reflect on the lesson of the bison. Why is it important to face challenges head-on? How can this philosophy be applied in both personal and professional settings?

Action Plan (10 minutes):

- Based on the discussions and reflections, ask each participant to jot down one commitment they're making to themselves. This should be a realistic action related to facing a current or future challenge head-on.

- If in a team setting, consider creating a team commitment or mantra based on the lesson of the bison.

Closure (5 minutes):

- Thank the participants for their openness and vulnerability.

- Remind everyone that just as the bison faces the storm, they too possess the innate strength to confront any adversity that comes their way. Encourage them to remember today's reflection whenever they're faced with a storm, and to always choose the path of the bison.

This reflective exercise serves as a reminder that while adversity is inevitable, how we approach it defines our growth and resilience. Facing challenges head-on not only builds character but also equips us with tools and experiences that enrich our journey through life.

Leaders: there are exercises like this at the end of several chapters. If you want to print off a PDF of the exercises to use with your team, go to intothestormbook.com/into-the-storm-exercises or scan this QR Code

CHAPTER 2: LESSONS FROM THE MEADOW

As the rain intensified, Alex and his father made their way to the old barn adjacent to their house. It was a place full of memories – from learning to build a birdhouse to secret hide-and-seek games with Grace. The barn, with its musty smell and dim lighting, had always been a refuge.

They settled on an old bench, the rain providing a rhythmic backdrop to their conversation. Alex's father began, "When I was about your age, Grandpa took me on a trip to Montana. It was there that I first came to understand the behavior of bison during storms."

Alex raised an eyebrow, intrigued. "I don't get it. What do bison and cows have to do with my knee or the storm?"

His father smiled, a hint of nostalgia in his eyes. "You see, while we were camping, a severe storm hit. We had to secure our tent and belongings, but I remember being captivated by the herd of bison in the distance."

He paused, collecting his thoughts. "Bison have a unique way of dealing with storms. Unlike cows that try to outrun or hide from them, bison face them head-on. They move into the storm. It's an instinctual behavior. By heading into the storm, they get through it faster. They still experience the difficulty of the storm, but by going into it they minimize the discomfort and duration."

Alex mulled over this, trying to find the relevance. "So you're saying I should... what? Head into my problems like a bison?"

"In a way, yes," his father replied. "But it's deeper than that. Let's break it down."

Lesson 1: You can't avoid the storm. "Adversity, Alex, is a part of life. Just like those storms in Montana or the one outside right now, challenges will come. Whether it's an injury, a bad grade, or a personal setback, you can't avoid them. The problem is most people don't expect adversity. They think life is just going to be easy. And when you don't expect adversity, you get surprised by it. The sooner you accept that adversity is inevitable, the better prepared and equipped you'll be to handle it, and the faster you'll get through it."

Alex shifted uncomfortably. "It just seems unfair, Dad. I was so close. Maybe I should just quit."

His father nodded. "That's an option, but that sounds like your emotions talking. And I get it, you're frustrated. I know it seems unfair. Life often feels that way. Fair isn't guaranteed. Nobody escapes adversity. It doesn't matter how good of a person you are, how many things you are doing right in your life. Adversity doesn't discriminate. But running from it won't make it better and won't make it go away. You have to realize that adversity doesn't happen to you, it happens for you. Think of the countless great personalities we look up to – athletes, scientists, leaders, adventurers – every one of them faced challenges. Most, even more daunting than mine or yours. Yet, their legacy isn't their setbacks; it's how they responded to them. They had a choice just like you do. To be a victim of adversity or to claim victory over it. Adversity is just part of the path. It's what you do with it that matters. If you use it well, adversity refines us. It makes us better."

Lesson 2: Trying to avoid the storm only makes things worse.

"I just wish it wasn't real," Alex sighed. "It feels like a nightmare."

"I know it does. And I'm sorry you're going through it. Sometimes you have to just keep chopping wood. It's not easy now and it won't be easy in the future. But there are lessons to be learned. When you first felt that pain in your leg, you tried to ignore it, hoping it'd go away on its own. The only thing that did was make it worse. You should've pulled out of practice earlier. Even at dinner, you were trying to avoid the issue, believing that the doctors got it wrong and that everything is fine. That's a natural reaction. But denial and avoidance can be harmful. Like the cow that believes it can outrun the storm, we often think we can escape our problems. But all that does is prolong our exposure to them, making them more difficult to overcome. You can't get out of the storm. You must choose to get through it. And believe that better days are always ahead. The sooner you accept that, the faster you can get moving forward."

Alex looked down, recalling the sharp stabs of pain he'd felt during practice. "I just wanted it to be a minor cramp that would work itself out," he mumbled.

"And that's okay," his father reassured. "I get it. Hindsight is always 20/20. And sometimes powering through is the right move. But that part is over. Now, it's essential to confront reality. Running from it won't change the diagnosis or speed up your recovery. You can't focus on the what if, you have to focus on the what now. The more you ignore it, the more difficult your situation becomes. Eventually, you're going to have to face it. To go head-first into dealing with it. It's just a matter of when."

The rain outside began to ease, transitioning into a gentle drizzle. The duo sat in silence, the weight of the conversation sinking in. It was a lot for Alex to process. His life had taken an unexpected turn, and he was grappling with the ramifications.

His father broke the silence, pointing to the far end of the meadow, where a group of deer had emerged, cautious and alert. "Nature has a rhythm, a cycle. After every storm, there's calm. After night, there's day. And after adversity, there's growth. If you use it the right way. It's all about perspective, and your perspective is a choice."

Alex glanced at his father, his eyes full of questions, yearning for guidance. Recognizing this, his father continued, "In the coming days, you'll have choices to make – about your rehab, your attitude, and your future. You can choose to be the cow, constantly trying to evade, or be the bison, facing challenges head-on. The choices you make will determine the future you create. How you respond is up to you."

Drawing a deep breath, Alex nodded, the weight of the decision bearing down on him. "I want to be the bison," he whispered, determination evident in his voice.

His father smiled, wrapping an arm around him. "And that's the first step."

As they left the barn, the storm had passed, leaving in its wake a glistening meadow, the scent of wet earth, and a rainbow arching across the sky. It was a new beginning, a fresh start. The lessons from the meadow had laid the foundation for Alex's journey of resilience, acceptance, and growth. The path ahead was uncertain, filled with challenges and unknowns. But with the wisdom of the bison to guide him, Alex was ready to face the storm. He knew that the only way through it was through it.

Reflection Exercise: Navigating The Consequences Of Avoidance

Objective: To help individuals or teams recognize the repercussions of avoiding challenges, using the second lesson that suggests "trying to avoid the storm only makes things worse."

Instructions:

Individual Reflection (10 minutes):

- Begin with a deep breathing exercise to help participants center themselves.

- Prompt each participant to think of a challenge or adversity they once avoided or delayed addressing.

- Invite them to remember the emotions associated with that avoidance – the anxiety, the relief of immediate avoidance, and the eventual confrontation.

Journaling (15 minutes):

- Ask participants to write down the challenge or adversity they avoided.

- Underneath, they should chronicle the reasons for their initial avoidance or delay.

- Encourage them to detail the eventual consequences of that delay. Did it lead to more significant problems or complications? How did it make them feel?

Group Sharing (If applicable, 20 minutes):

- Create a safe environment for participants to share their experiences without judgment.

- As they share their avoidance stories, listen for common themes or emotions.

- Encourage feedback, support, and shared experiences among the group. The aim is to create mutual understanding and empathy.

Group Discussion (15 minutes):

- Discuss the natural human tendency to avoid discomfort and why this might not always be the best approach.

- Explore the long-term effects of avoidance. How does constantly running from challenges shape our character and life experiences?

- Reflect on the lesson: "Trying to avoid the storm only makes things worse." How does this resonate with the group's personal or professional experiences?

Action Plan (10 minutes):

- Based on the discussions and reflections, ask each participant to identify one current challenge they've been avoiding.

- Request them to outline a step-by-step plan to address that challenge in the coming weeks. This plan should be realistic and actionable.

- For team settings, consider a collective commitment where the team decides to address a shared challenge they've been avoiding.

Closure (5 minutes):

- Express gratitude to the participants for their honesty and participation.

- Remind them that while the initial discomfort of facing a challenge can be daunting, the long-term benefits of addressing it promptly far outweigh the temporary relief of avoidance. Encourage them to carry the lesson forward in their lives.

Through this exercise, participants will gain insight into their patterns of avoidance and the subsequent consequences. Recognizing these patterns is the first step towards breaking them and fostering a proactive approach to life's challenges.

CHAPTER 3: OUTRUNNING THE RAIN

Alex's days soon took on a predictable rhythm: school, physical therapy, homework, repeat. The buzzing school hallways, which once felt vibrant and alive with friends and anticipation of the next soccer match, now seemed more of a reminder of what he had lost. Whispers of his injury echoed around him, and Alex felt increasingly isolated from his peers.

One day, as he limped his way through the hallway, he overheard his teammates discussing the upcoming matches, the game plan to win, and the colleges scouting them. Alex's shoulder slumped and his eyes found the floor in front of him. Feeling a twinge of jealousy and bitterness, he quickened his pace, eager to escape the conversation.

That evening, his best friend, Mia, dropped by. Mia, the school's star swimmer, had faced her fair share of challenges too – from family drama to suffering and recovering from a shoulder injury the previous year. Yet, her spirit remained undeterred.

"Hey!" she greeted, holding up a board game. "Thought we could play something, maybe take your mind off things?"

Alex smirked, "Trying to distract me from my misery, huh?"

Mia laughed, "That's what friends are for. Plus, I brought cookies!"

As they set up the game, Mia noticed Alex's withdrawn demeanor. "You can't keep outrunning these feelings, Alex. Believe me, I've tried."

Alex looked up, a mixture of confusion and curiosity evident in his eyes. Mia sighed, recalling her own journey of overcoming. "After my shoulder injury, I tried to distract myself in every way possible. I immersed myself in books, movies, social media, whatever I could do to take my mind off of my situation. But every time I saw a pool or heard about a swim meet, the pain returned. It was overwhelming at times."

She paused, letting the gravity of her words sink in. "The thing is, by avoiding our feelings, we give them more power. Sooner or later, they catch up to us. If we don't control our feelings, they will control us. We become what we think about. The more I focused on my frustration, the more frustrated I became. The more I focused on making progress, the more I made progress. Eventually I learned that it didn't matter how I felt. I got to choose how I showed up each day. When I took ownership of my attitude, things got better."

Alex leaned back, absorbing Mia's words. "Like a cow,

running from the storm," he realized. Mia had a confused look on her face so Alex had to explain the lesson his dad had shared about the bison and the cow. He realized he had been doing precisely that: running away. Every time soccer was mentioned, he'd change the conversation or leave the room. He'd stopped wearing his team jacket and even avoided watching games on TV. He had been running, trying to escape the reality of his situation. He was letting his feelings control him. He had committed to being like the bison but was starting to realize how hard it is. And that it's not just in one situation, it is in every situation.

Lesson 2: "Trying to avoid the storm only makes things worse." His father's words echoed in his mind. He looked at Mia and curiously asked. "How did you do it? How did you stop running from the problem and the feelings?"

Mia smiled, "I faced it. I learned that adversity isn't about what's on the outside, it's about what is happening on the inside. It's about who you are, your character, determination, mindset, resilience. I couldn't control the problem but I could control myself. Facing adversity is about living your standard, not your feelings. I started attending swim meets as a spectator, cheered for my teammates, and slowly, the bitterness waned. It wasn't easy, and it didn't happen overnight. But by confronting my feelings, I robbed them of their power. Our feelings don't have to determine how we show up. We don't always control our circumstances, but we control how we respond to them. Once I started responding in a better way, my situation got better. I could choose to be negative or positive, to be bitter or be excited for my teammates, to be selfish or be a great teammate. The truth was there were a lot of good things going on in my life. I decided to focus on those. When I chose a better attitude and perspective, everything got better."

Alex pondered this, the weight of the realization heavy on his shoulders. "I've been running, haven't I?"

Mia nodded, "But recognizing it is the first step. Now, you've got to face it."

With renewed determination, Alex decided to attend the next soccer match. He stood on the sidelines, wearing his team jacket, cheering for his friends. Every goal, every pass, was bittersweet. It wasn't easy, but he chose to be positive and supportive. But as the match progressed, he felt a shift. "I get to choose my response. Have a bison mentality," he said to himself. The weight of resentment was lifting, replaced by pride for his team and hope for his future.

The journey was far from over. There were days when despair threatened to overwhelm him, moments when the storm clouds seemed unending, times when he wondered what the point of all of it was and wanted to quit. But with each step, Alex was learning. He was no longer the cow, attempting to evade the storm. He was the bison, facing it head-on, learning, growing, and emerging stronger. As a reminder, he put a post it note on the mirror in his bathroom to give him the mindset he needed each day: "Be a bison."

As the days turned into weeks, Alex's rehab progressed. His physical therapist commended his dedication, and slowly, he began to regain strength and mobility. The dream of returning to the soccer field wasn't as distant as it once seemed.

As it goes with adversity, Alex wasn't always in a good mood. He wasn't always hopeful or full of belief.

During one session, after a particularly rough day, Alex found himself complaining. "Why do I even do this?" he questioned. "Sometimes I wonder if it's even worth it."

"You actually have a lot to be grateful for," his PT noted. "What are you talking about?" Alex said with a tone of frustration.

"No matter what's happening in life, we can always choose gratitude. It's about your perspective. Think about it. Give me 5 things in your life that you are grateful for."

Alex grumbled. "Fine. My family. My friends. Food. My bed. My mom driving me here." He didn't want to admit it, but he could sense his mood improving.

His physical therapist then introduced him to the concept of gratitude journaling, explaining how it could transform his perspective during this tough time. Initially, Alex was skeptical. The idea of writing down things he was grateful for seemed trivial compared to the magnitude of his struggles. Yet, he couldn't deny the persistent feeling of negativity that clouded his days. Willing to try anything that might help, he decided to give it a shot.

Every night before bed, Alex began to jot down three things he was grateful for in a small notebook. The first few entries were simple and somewhat strained - things like "a sunny day" or "a good meal." But as the days progressed, he found himself noticing and appreciating small joys he had previously overlooked. The warmth of a conversation with a friend, the progress in his rehab, even the comfort of his favorite hoodie. This practice of acknowledging the positive aspects of his life, no matter how small, slowly started to shift his mindset.

Alongside gratitude journaling, Alex began to consciously adopt a more positive perspective. When negative thoughts crept in, he challenged them, searching for a silver lining. In his rehab, instead of dwelling on the exercises he couldn't do, he focused on the progress he was making. When he felt isolated from his team, he reminded himself of the support and camaraderie they still offered off the field.

This shift didn't happen overnight, and there were days when positivity seemed like a distant dream. Yet, Alex persisted, and over time, these practices became a cornerstone of his recovery. Gratitude journaling and choosing positivity didn't just help him cope with his injury; they redefined his approach to life's challenges. He learned that while he couldn't control the adversity he faced, he could control his response to it. These mental toughness practices illuminated a path of resilience and hope, guiding Alex towards not just recovery, but personal growth and a renewed zest for life.

One day, after an intense rehab session, Mia and Alex sat on his porch, eating her now-famous cookies. The horizon was painted with hues of pink and gold, a gentle reminder that every storm runs out of rain.

"Remember our first swim race?" Mia asked, a playful glint in her eye.

Alex laughed, "How could I forget? You beat me by a mile!"

Mia grinned, "That's because I wasn't running from the rain; I was swimming through it."

"That might be the worst joke I've ever heard," Alex laughingly responded. They both laughed, their bond deepened by shared struggles and resilience. The path ahead was uncertain, but Alex knew one thing for sure – he wasn't alone in his journey. With the support of loved ones and the wisdom of the bison, he was ready to face any storm that came his way.

Reflection Exercise: Gratitude Is The Way

Objective: To cultivate a positive mindset and enhance team cohesion by recognizing and appreciating the positive aspects of daily life.

Instructions:

Individual Reflection (5 minutes):

- Ask participants to spend 5 minutes writing down three things they are grateful for. These can be personal or related to work/school, and can include small moments or significant events. Remind them that no matter how difficult the current situation may be, there is always something to be grateful for.

- Encourage them to be specific and to reflect on why they are grateful for each item.

Group Sharing (If applicable, and optional, 15 minutes):

- If working with a team, invite someone to share one item from their gratitude list. This can help build a sense of community and provide inspiration to others. Continue until everyone who wishes to share has the opportunity.

Daily Practice (5 minutes):

- Encourage participants to make this a daily habit. Suggest setting aside a few minutes each day, either in the morning or before bed, to jot down three things they are grateful for.

This exercise is designed to be simple yet powerful, helping individuals and teams build resilience and a positive mindset through the practice of gratitude.

CHAPTER 4: FINDING YOUR HERD

Rehabilitation was a long, arduous journey. There were exercises that tested Alex's patience, sessions that wrung tears of frustration from him, and moments where he questioned whether he'd ever play soccer again. Quitting crossed his mind often, but he kept going. Through it all, one thing became abundantly clear: the company you keep plays a pivotal role in your journey through adversity.

Initially, Alex felt isolated. Many friends from the soccer team, preoccupied with their schedules and the ongoing season, seldom checked on him. But as days rolled on, a pattern emerged. Mia was a constant pillar of support, often sharing her experiences and pep talks. Classmates made sure he had what he needed to get to and from class. And to Alex's surprise, Coach Williams, his team's stern and no-nonsense coach, visited him weekly, updating him on the team's progress and discussing strategies. After a while, a few of his closest teammates began to show up. They'd acknowledged they didn't really know how to handle it at first but ultimately wanted to be great teammates and friends, knowing that they wouldn't want to go through the same situation alone if it had been them.

One afternoon, as Alex grappled with a particularly tough PT session, he felt a hand on his shoulder. Looking up, he saw his coach's familiar stern face, but his eyes held a softness Alex had rarely seen before.

"Mind if I join?" Coach Williams asked, taking a seat beside Alex.

Taken aback by the sight of his coach, Alex nodded, "Of course, Coach. What brings you here?"

Coach Williams sighed, "When I was in high school, I blew out my knee. It was the end of my playing career. I wasn't as careful with it as I should have been, so I have to do the work to take care of it today."

Coach Williams, known for his unwavering strength and inspirational speeches, hadn't always been the epitome of resilience. He explained to Alex that his journey had been marked by a series of struggles that shaped him into the mentor he is today. In his early days, Williams was a promising athlete, his future in soccer shining brightly. However, during his senior year of high school, a devastating knee injury shattered his dreams of playing professionally. The incident plunged him into a period of despair, as the identity he had built around being an athlete crumbled.

For years, Williams grappled with this loss, his sense of purpose wavering. He took odd jobs, often finding himself reminiscing about what could have been. It was during this period of aimlessness that he stumbled upon a youth league in need of a coach. Reluctant at first, he soon discovered a newfound passion in coaching. He realized that while his path as an athlete had ended, his journey in sports had not. Coaching became his solace and redemption, a way to channel his love for the game and impact young lives. The lessons he learned from his own adversity - resilience, adaptability, and the power of a positive mindset - became the cornerstone of his coaching philosophy. "I wouldn't be who I am today or doing what I'm doing today without all of those moments," he explained.

Alex stared, dumbfounded. He'd never known this side of his coach's story. "But... you never mentioned..."

Coach Williams gave a slight smile, "It's not something I broadcast. But I thought it might help you to know you're not alone in this."

Their conversation meandered from soccer to life, challenges, and recovery. Coach Williams shared his journey, the despair he felt, and how he channeled his passion for the game into coaching. "It wasn't easy, Alex," he admitted, "But my family, my teammates – they became my herd. They shielded me from the harshest elements of the struggle and showed me that there was life beyond the injury. Sometimes they even protected me from myself and my own negative mindset. With the right people around you, you can get through anything. We all need trusted truth-tellers in our life."

Lesson 3: There is power in the herd. "The herd," Alex thought out loud. "Interesting. Just like the bison running into the storm together. They have the right herd."

"I see your dad has finally told you his story of the bison and the cows?" Coach laughed. "But he's right. Just as bison huddle together, facing storms as a unified force, we humans too draw strength from our community. Your 'herd' can be your family, friends, teammates, or even people who've walked a similar path. But it's not just about having a herd, it's about the right herd. The wrong herd can steer you in the wrong direction, making your situation even worse. If I had had the wrong people in my life, who knows what horrible path I might've gone down. Following the wrong voices, like the cows, will lead you down the wrong path. The voices we listen to impact the choices we make. Better voices lead to better choices. You have to surround yourself with the right people in order to get where you want to go in life."

Over the next few weeks, Alex began to recognize his 'herd.' Mia, always ready with a joke or encouragement. His father, sharing life lessons and wisdom. Coach Williams, providing guidance and perspective. His mom and sister always being supportive and understanding. His friends and teammates, there when he needed them the most.

One day, as Alex sat with Mia and a few friends in his living room, engrossed in a movie, a realization dawned upon him. While the injury was undeniably a setback, it had also brought unexpected blessings. It sifted out fair-weather friends and highlighted those who genuinely cared. There were moments in the process where he felt alone and overwhelmed, but the truth is that he had people alongside him the whole time.

"Finding your herd isn't just about seeking comfort," his father mused one morning over breakfast, "It's about surrounding yourself with those who push you to be better, who challenge you, and who stand by you, come rain or shine. You need a herd who will run into the storm with you. Who won't let you give up when things get difficult."

As the days turned into weeks, Alex's 'herd' became his fortress. Their collective strength, wisdom, and support acted as a buffer, helping him navigate the tumultuous waters of recovery, physically and mentally.

By the time the first snowflakes of winter began to fall, Alex was back on his feet, walking without a limp. His return to the soccer field was still a few months away, but with his newfound perspective, he was in no hurry. He had learned the value of patience, resilience, and, most importantly, the strength of community.

Sitting on his porch, a mug of hot chocolate in hand, Alex gazed out at the vast meadow, now blanketed in snow. The bison analogy, which initially seemed like just a quirky lesson from his father, had come to define his journey. And as the snowflakes danced around him, he felt an overwhelming sense of gratitude. For the storm, for the lessons, but most importantly, for his herd.

Reflection Exercise: The Strength Of Your Herd

Objective: To help individuals or teams understand and value the influence of those around them, drawing from the third lesson: "There is power in the herd."

Instructions:

Individual Reflection (10 minutes):

- Start with a moment of silence to let participants collect their thoughts.

- Prompt each person to think about their current 'herd' – the friends, family, mentors, and colleagues who influence their daily life.

- Ask them to reflect on the positive influences and support they've received from this group, as well as any challenges or negative influences they might have experienced.

Mapping Your Herd (15 minutes):

- Give each participant a few small cards or sticky notes.

- On each card, ask them to write down the name of someone significant in their life and a word or phrase that encapsulates that person's influence (e.g., "Sara - Encouragement" or "Mike - Doubt").

- Once they've created a card for each influential person, participants should spread them out in front of them, placing positive influences on one side and challenging influences on the other.

Group Sharing (If applicable, 20 minutes):

- Ask participants to share some of the key members of their 'herd' and the influences they've noted.

- Encourage open dialogue about the benefits of positive influences and strategies for managing or mitigating challenging ones.

- Create a safe environment where participants feel comfortable discussing personal relationships, reminding them of the importance of confidentiality.

Group Discussion (15 minutes):

- Delve into the broader topic of how the people we surround ourselves with shape our thoughts, actions, and overall well-being.

- Discuss strategies for seeking out and nurturing positive relationships and distancing oneself from toxic or negative influences.

- Reflect on the group or team's collective 'herd'. Are there shared influences that impact everyone? How can the group work together to bolster each other during challenging times?

Action Plan (10 minutes):

- Ask each participant to identify one or two steps they can take to strengthen their 'herd' – this could be deepening a positive relationship, seeking a mentor, or setting boundaries with a challenging influence.

- Encourage them to write these steps down and commit to taking action in the next month.

- For teams, discuss how you can collectively support and empower each other. Perhaps establish regular check-ins or team-building activities.

Closure (5 minutes):

- Thank everyone for their openness and trust.

- Reiterate the importance of cultivating and valuing the 'herd'. Encourage participants to be intentional about the company they keep, reminding them of the profound impact these relationships can have on their journey through life's many storms.

This exercise is designed to foster self-awareness about the influence of relationships, highlighting the immense power that a supportive 'herd' can bring to an individual's life.

CHAPTER 5: THE RAINBOW AFTER THE RAIN

Winter melted into spring, and with each passing day, Alex's determination to get back on the field intensified. His physical strength was returning, and every physical therapy session brought him closer to his goal. But what had transformed more profoundly was his mindset. He had learned lessons of resilience, of commitment, about choosing your perspective. Something Coach Williams had said stuck with him. "Adversity is inevitable, growth is optional."

One balmy afternoon, as he practiced dribbling in his backyard, a soccer ball rolled over from the neighboring fence. A small, red-haired boy, no older than twelve, scampered after it. Recognizing Alex, his eyes widened in awe. "You're Alex Harris! I watched you play last season. You're amazing!"

Alex chuckled, "Thanks, bud. Wish I could've played the whole season. What's your name?"

"Jamie," the boy replied, admiration evident in his eyes.

As they talked, Alex learned that Jamie had recently moved to the neighborhood and was facing challenges of his own. Starting at a new school, trying to make friends, and all that came with being a new kid in a new town was taking a toll on the young boy's spirit. "It's tough being the new kid," Jamie explained.

Remembering his father's lessons and his recent experiences, Alex shared the story of the bison and the cow. Jamie listened intently, drawing parallels between his challenges and the approaching storm. "I'm not saying it will be easy, but I've got your back," Alex encouraged. "You don't have to face this alone. We'll get through the storm together."

By the end of their conversation, Jamie looked visibly uplifted. "Thanks, Alex," he beamed, "I'll be a bison. I promise." After a fist bump, he continued on his way.

Alex smiled, realizing the ripple effect of resilience and the power of shared stories. His journey of recovery had equipped him with wisdom and perspective, which he could now share with others.

Lesson 4: Every storm runs out of rain. Just as Jamie left, Mia dropped by with cookies. Suddenly the phone rang. Alex answered it and couldn't believe what he was hearing. "Are you serious? This isn't a joke? Thank you!" Hanging up, he exclaimed to Mia, "I'm cleared! I get to start training with the team next week! Let's go!"

Overwhelmed with emotion, Alex hugged Mia. The journey that began with despair was nearing its hopeful culmination. His family came in from the next room after overhearing the celebration. Alex looked at his parents and embraced them with big hugs. "Did you hear that? I'm cleared!"

His mom and sister had tears welling up in their eyes. His dad smiled. "Congrats, son. Every storm runs out of rain and your storm looks like it has ended. Adversity has its season. I know you thought it might never end, but the storm always passes. Too often, when adversity hits, we put a frame around the situation and believe this is how things will always be. That this will be the whole story. The truth is that it's just part of our story. The key is for us to have perspective, to remember that light always follows the dark. Which means even during hard seasons, we must not lose hope. While hope isn't a good strategy, it is a powerful fuel that can keep us going during difficult days. And that's exactly what you did. I'm proud of you."

Returning to the field, however, was more challenging than he had anticipated. He was out of sync with his teammates, his movements lacked the fluidity of the past, and self-doubt began to creep in.

But then he remembered the bison. He remembered the lessons from the meadow, his determination to face adversity, the power of his herd, and the promise that every storm would eventually run out of rain. 'I've got this," he said to himself. Each day, he pushed himself a little harder, leaning on his teammates for support and guidance. His dad's voice echoed in his mind, "The struggle is where you develop your strength."

One evening, after an exhausting practice session, Coach Williams pulled Alex aside. "You're making good progress," he said, his voice gruff but sincere. "Remember, it's not about how fast you get there. It's about the journey and what you learn along the way. Progress is a process. Be patient with it. Something I like to remember is the power of yet. When you get frustrated that you aren't where you want to be, just add on a 'yet' to the end of it. You aren't where you want to be, yet. It's a reminder that you aren't a finished product."

Alex nodded, taking solace in Coach's words. His return to competitive soccer was a month away, and he was determined to make the most of it.

Lesson 5: Do hard things. As the days progressed, this lesson became Alex's mantra. Whether it was pushing through a grueling workout, confronting his fears on the field, or helping Jamie navigate the challenges of a new school, Alex was committed to building his mental toughness, or what he called the Bison Mentality. The note on his mirror was becoming reality. He had even set reminders throughout the day on his phone to remind him of who he was becoming and to re-center his thoughts on being positive and controlling what he could control. Every day at 9:00a his phone buzzed, "I can do hard things." At 11:30, he got a reminder that "Adversity is about how you respond." At 2:00p, "I am resilient." And at 7:30p, "I've got this." Noticing the change in him, his teammates had joined in this practice as well.

A sports psychologist who worked at his training and rehab facility had told him that training isn't just for the body, it's for the mind. He had given him exercises to do to build confidence, resilience and a strong mindset. "Think of it this way. Everybody has two forces in their mind that are competing for their attention, their attitude, their efforts. Those forces are the Critic and the Champion. The Critic is that voice that tells you to make excuses, to take the easy way out, to give up. It constantly tries to get you not to do the things you know you need to do. The Champion, though, is telling you that you can do hard things, it is pushing you in the right direction and holding you accountable. It is the voice of discipline, commitment and belief. Which voice we listen to, the Critic or the Champion, shapes the choices we make, the actions we take and the person we become. Too many listen to the Critic every day. It causes them to avoid discomfort. Which means whenever life throws them an obstacle, they don't know how to handle it. They continue listening to the Critic which leads to complaining, making excuses, and giving up. The only way to get better at doing hard things is to do hard things. To quiet the Critic. To listen to the Champion in order to become the Champion. Remember that the first battle to win is the one in your mind. Everything begins with how you think. The best learn to train their mind in order to make their mindset their advantage."

Finally, the day of his return to competitive soccer arrived. The stadium buzzed with excitement. Sitting in the locker room before the match, Alex felt his phone buzz. It was a text from his dad with a storm and bison emojis that read, "Bison Mentality."

As Alex stepped onto the field, the crowd erupted in cheers. Every pass, every move was met with anticipation. The match was intense, and as the final whistle blew, Alex's team emerged victorious.

But for Alex, the victory was more personal. It was a testament to his journey, the challenges he faced, and the lessons he learned. As he celebrated with his teammates and coaches, he spotted his family, Mia, and even Jamie in the stands, cheering him on. They were his herd, his anchor through the storm.

That evening, as they all gathered at Alex's house for a celebratory dinner, his father raised a toast. "To Alex," he began, his voice filled with pride, "who showed us the power of resilience, the importance of community, and the promise that every storm, no matter how fierce, will eventually run out of rain. A true embodiment of the Bison Mentality."

The room echoed with cheers and applause, but Alex's thoughts were introspective. He had emerged from the storm, not just stronger, but wiser. And as he looked out of the window, he noticed a rainbow arching across the sky – a vivid reminder of the beauty that follows adversity. As Coach Williams liked to say, "Everything good is on the other side of adversity."

In the days that followed, Alex continued to shine on the soccer field, but his impact would extend far beyond it. He now had a story to tell, a message to give. He wanted people to know that adversity was normal, that the key is in how you respond to it.

Life was filled with its share of challenges, but Alex was undeterred. He had faced the storm, found his herd, and emerged with wisdom that can only come from the battle. And as he journeyed forward, he carried the lessons of the bison, the promise of brighter days, and the unyielding spirit of resilience in his heart.

Reflection Exercise: Finding Hope Amidst The Storm

Objective: To inspire individuals or teams to adopt a perspective that even the most daunting adversities are temporary, resonating with the lesson: "Every storm runs out of rain."

Instructions:

Guided Imagery (10 minutes):

- Request participants to sit comfortably and close their eyes.
- Guide them through a calming breathing exercise to set the tone.
- Now, invite them to imagine a heavy rainstorm. Let them visualize the dark clouds, the torrential rain, and the intense wind.
- Slowly, guide them to visualize the rain lessening, the winds dying down, and the clouds beginning to part, revealing a gentle light or a rainbow.
- After the imagery, ask them to return to their breathing and then gradually open their eyes.

Individual Reflection (10 minutes):

- After the guided imagery, ask participants to think of a challenging time in their life that felt like a never-ending storm but eventually passed.
- Encourage them to recall how they felt during the adversity and how they felt once it had passed.

Journaling (15 minutes):

- Participants should write down the challenging time they recalled.

- Below that, they should note how they felt during the challenge and the feelings or realizations they experienced after the adversity passed.

- Ask them to reflect on any lessons or growth that emerged from that challenging time.

Group Sharing (If applicable, 20 minutes):

- In a safe and supportive environment, invite participants to share their experiences of the storms in their life and the eventual sunlight they found.

- This is an opportunity for empathy, understanding, and mutual support. Encourage active listening and gentle feedback.

Group Discussion (15 minutes):

- Engage in a conversation about the impermanent nature of challenges and adversities.

- Reflect on strategies or coping mechanisms that help individuals hold on to hope during tough times.

- Discuss the value of perspective and how reminding oneself that "every storm runs out of rain" can be a source of strength during adversity.

Action Plan (10 minutes):

- Have participants think of a current challenge they're facing or anticipate facing.

- Ask them to write down three reminders or affirmations they can use to help themselves remember the temporary nature of this challenge. For example, "This too shall pass," or "Every challenge is an opportunity for growth."

- In team settings, consider creating a collective affirmation that the team can use during challenging times or projects.

Closure (5 minutes):

- Express gratitude for the courage and openness displayed during the exercise.

- Reiterate the invaluable lesson that while adversities are inevitable, they are also temporary. Encourage participants to carry this perspective with them, drawing strength from the knowledge that sunlight always follows the rain.

This exercise reinforces the belief in hope and resilience, enabling participants to face adversities with a renewed perspective and optimism.

CHAPTER 6: NAVIGATING LIFE'S STORMS

Under the vast expanse of the evening sky, the soccer field was more than just a stretch of green; it was a place of transformation. Here, amidst the echoes of games past, Alex found himself in the role of a mentor to Sam, a freshman whose life's storms drew him to Alex, someone he had seen weather such storms with resilience and grit. Alex had always been a leader on the team, but now he was taking the role to a new level.

Their sessions began just messing around with the soccer ball, but quickly evolved into something far deeper. Alex saw in Sam a raw potential, not just in soccer, but in life. He recognized the familiar look of struggle in Sam's eyes – the same look he'd had during his toughest days. "Adversity is normal," Alex explained. "I've realized it's just part of life. It doesn't discriminate. Sooner or later, we all face it. What matters is what we do with it."

One late afternoon, as they worked through drills, Alex

introduced Sam to the concept of a daily mantra. "Words have power, Sam. Your self-talk can be your armor against the world's chaos," Alex said, sharing his own mantra, "I can do hard things." "I think you should come up with one. Something simple to remind you that you're able to handle anything you face. Because here's what I've come to understand since my injury. Adversity isn't about what's going on around you, it's about what is within you. In order to overcome adversity, we must build a resilient mindset. When we're full of worry, negativity, doubt and fear, we shrink back. But when we're hopeful, positive, confident, and believe, we can take on any adversity. How we think determines how we act. But a strong mindset doesn't happen by accident. Our mind is a muscle, and the more we work at it the stronger it gets. The more we ignore it, the weaker it gets."

"I never thought of it that way," Sam replied. "I just thought people were magically confident. Saying that out loud now, I guess it sounds ridiculous. But if a strong mindset is available to everybody, that's a game changer."

The next time they met, Alex brought up the concept again, asking if Sam had come up with anything. "Yeah, but I'm embarrassed to share it," he said quietly. "I get it, man. It can be a little weird. But there's nothing to be embarrassed about. Especially if it helps you. So what is it?"

"I am a winner," Sam said with minimum confidence. "I like it. Go deeper, explain it to me," said Alex. "Well, I feel like with everything going on, I need to remind myself that I won't be defeated. That I'm a winner. And whatever I face, I will beat it. I won't let it win." The confidence was building in Sam as he gave the reason behind his daily mantra. "I love it!" Alex said with encouragement. "That's perfect. You are a winner."

As their bond deepened, Alex introduced Sam to the idea of the inner critic and champion. "Inside each of us, there's a critic that dwells on our fears and failures, and a champion that celebrates our strengths and successes," Alex explained one cool evening. He shared stories of his own battles with self-doubt, and how learning to listen to his inner champion helped him overcome them. "I've learned that most people give too much power to their Critic and it holds them back. When we empower the Champion, we unlock our strength."

In turn, Sam opened up about his own critic, the voice that magnified his fears about his parents' separation and his sense of belonging. Together, they worked on exercises to recognize and counter the critic's voice. Alex would have Sam voice out his criticisms and then counter them with positive affirmations, slowly helping him to amplify his inner champion. "We must counter the lies with truth," Alex explained. "Otherwise the lies win. The more we speak truth to ourself, the more our mind changes. We start to be transformed by the renewing of our mind."

Alex introduced Sam to the concept of an adversity scale, an exercise to help put his problems into perspective. "Imagine a scale from one to ten, one being a minor inconvenience, ten being a life-altering challenge. Where do your current problems fit?" Alex asked during one of their sessions.

This exercise helped Sam understand that not all problems required the same emotional energy or response. He learned to assess situations more objectively, reducing the overwhelming feelings that often accompanied his thoughts.

On a cloudy afternoon, with a storm brewing in the distance, Alex spoke about the power of visualization. "Picture yourself succeeding, Sam. Visualize overcoming your challenges, just like we visualize winning a game. See yourself as the bison running into the storm, not the cow running away from the storm," he advised.

They would spend the first few minutes of their sessions visualizing their goals – Sam seeing himself excelling in soccer and finding peace at home, Alex envisioning his continued growth as a mentor and leader. This practice of visualization became a cornerstone of their meetings, instilling a sense of hope and direction.

Alex knew that theory alone wasn't enough. He designed practical exercises for Sam, tasks that pushed him out of his comfort zone. One such task was the 'Conversation Challenge,' where Sam had to initiate conversations with new people each day, building his confidence in unfamiliar situations.

Another exercise was the 'Gratitude Walk.' Together, they would walk around the field, each step accompanied by something they were grateful for. This simple exercise helped Sam shift his focus from his problems to the positives in his life.

After a few weeks of working together, Alex and Sam took time to reflect on their journey. They revisited their initial conversations, noting the growth in Sam's attitude and confidence. "It's important to celebrate progress," Alex said. "To look back on how far we've come gives us confidence to keep going." Alex felt a swell of pride seeing the young boy who once carried the weight of the world on his shoulders now standing taller, his eyes bright with newfound resilience.

"Life will throw many challenges at you, Sam. Remember, like the bison, face them head-on. And always know, you're not alone in this. You've got a herd behind and with you."

They walked off the field that day as different people than when they first started together. Sam, armed with lessons of resilience and the support of his mentor, was now ready to face life's storms with the true bison mentality. And Alex, having imparted his wisdom, felt a renewed sense of purpose, knowing he had made a difference in the life of another.

CHAPTER 7: THE BISON MENTALITY PROGRAM

The air was crisp and energizing as Alex walked the familiar paths of the school. His mind was abuzz with ideas, fueled by the success of his mentorship with Sam. Inspired by this transformation, Alex was determined to expand the reach of his lessons on resilience and mental toughness. He envisioned a program that would encapsulate the essence of their journey and extend it to the entire school. The Bison Mentality Program, as he decided to call it, would be a tribute to the lessons learned and a beacon of hope and strength for all students.

Alex approached Sam and Mia with his idea, and their enthusiasm was immediate. Mia, with her own journey of overcoming personal challenges, brought a perspective that was both insightful and inspiring. Sam, now a living testament to the power of these lessons, was eager to share his experience with others. Together, they began laying the groundwork for the Bison Mentality Program.

Alex, Sam, and Mia decided that the program would be structured around the five main lessons, each designed to help students build confidence and mental toughness to handle adversity:

Lesson 1: You can't avoid the storm. Just as the sun guarantees the day and the moon heralds the night, adversity is a guarantee in life. We cannot run from it, nor can we wish it away. It will come, as surely as the changing seasons.

Lesson 2: Trying to avoid the storm only makes things worse. Much like the cow that tries to outrun the storm and ends up spending more time in the rain, evading challenges only amplifies them. The storm will catch up, and when it does, it finds us exhausted, unprepared, and still drenched. The only way through it is through it.

Lesson 3: There is power in the herd. In isolation, we are vulnerable. But united, with a supportive community around us – be it friends, family, or mentors – we have the collective strength to face any storm.

Lesson 4: Every storm runs out of rain. This too shall pass. No matter how daunting the adversity, it is but a temporary phase. It is not the whole of our story, just a chapter in it. A season. The skies will clear, and the sun will shine again.

Lesson 5: Do hard things. To truly brace ourselves for life's storms, we must venture out into the rain deliberately, challenge ourselves, and build our resilience. It's in the act of facing adversity that we learn how to triumph over it. This is where your mindset is critical. You will face adversity in life. You will get knocked down. How you think determines how you respond. Mental toughness is about getting up one more time than you've been knocked down. Resilience comes from doing hard things.

With a clear vision, the trio presented their proposal to the school administration. Their passion and the transformative potential of the Bison Mentality Program won them immediate approval. They began organizing the inaugural session, which would be open to the entire student body.

The day of the first session arrived with a buzz of excitement. The school auditorium was filled with students, curious and eager to learn what the Bison Mentality Program was all about. Alex, Sam, and Mia stood on stage, a united front ready to share their vision. Jamie, inspired by his friend and neighbor Alex, sat in the front row.

Alex took the lead, sharing his story and the principles behind the Bison Mentality. He spoke about the inevitability of adversity and the power of facing it head-on. His words resonated with the students, many of whom were facing their own storms.

Sam shared his personal transformation, his voice ringing with sincerity and conviction. He spoke of the loneliness and confusion he felt during his parents' separation and how the mentorship with Alex had given him the tools to face his challenges.

Mia, with her natural empathy and insight, talked about the power of perspective. She shared her own struggles and how changing her outlook had helped her overcome them. Her message was clear: perspective is a choice, and a positive one can change everything.

The program was designed to be interactive, with activities that encouraged participation and self-reflection. One such activity was the 'Storm Simulation,' where students were presented with hypothetical challenging situations and asked to brainstorm solutions, applying the Bison Mentality principles.

Another key component was the 'Build Your Herd,' where students formed small groups to discuss their challenges and offer each other support and advice. This exercise not only fostered a sense of community but also helped students realize they were not alone in their struggles.

After every session, the trio would get together to discuss what went well and what could be better. They realized that teaching these lessons to a large group was a much more difficult task than working 1:1. While they felt as though they struggled a bit out of the gate, they were getting more comfortable speaking and teaching to the large group, and the students were being responsive. What they lacked in technical skills, they made up for in passion and authenticity. They leaned on teachers to help them come up with even more engaging exercises, and to get tips on structuring sessions to make them as impactful as possible. "Power in the herd, right?" noted Mia.

As the weeks passed, the Bison Mentality Program gained momentum. More students joined, drawn by the positive feedback and the visible changes in their peers. The program began to foster a culture of resilience and support within the school, changing the way students approached their challenges.

The impact of the program extended beyond the school walls. Students started applying the Bison Mentality principles in their homes, showcasing their newfound resilience. Teachers and parents noticed the difference – students were more engaged, confident, and better equipped to handle the ups and downs of life.

Alex, Sam, and Mia looked back on the journey of the Bison Mentality Program with pride and satisfaction. They had created something that went beyond themselves, a legacy that would continue to empower and inspire long after they had graduated.

In the final session, Alex addressed the auditorium filled with students who had grown in ways they never imagined. "Remember," he said, "life's storms don't define you. They refine you. Adversity is happening for you. Embrace it with the Bison Mentality, and you'll emerge stronger on the other side."

As the students filed out of the auditorium, there was a sense of unity and strength among them. They were no longer just individuals facing their storms alone; they were a herd, resilient and unbreakable, ready to face whatever life threw their way.

Sitting at home that night, Alex was filled with pride at the impact of the program. "Your adversity is never just about you," his dad noted. "It's always about taking what you learn to help somebody else. Using your struggles for good, sharing your lessons with others."

"I guess I have you to thank for all of this, dad. Your lessons were more important than I realized."

His dad smiled, "Turns out we can learn a thing or two from bison and cows."

CHAPTER 8: THE FINAL GAME

The sun cast a golden hue across the soccer field, its rays reflecting off the freshly painted white lines. The stadium, abuzz with excitement, was filled to capacity. Banners fluttered, drums echoed, and chants resonated, creating an electric atmosphere. It was the championship game. But this wasn't just any championship match – it was Alex's final game.

Over the years, Alex had faced numerous challenges on and off the field. Each storm, each obstacle, had shaped him into the player and person he was today. And as he laced up his boots, memories flashed before his eyes.

Lesson 1: You can't avoid the storm. From his first injury, the doubts that had plagued him, to the challenges Mia faced, and their collective journey towards the importance of mindset, storms had been an integral part of Alex's journey. They reminded him of his vulnerabilities, but more importantly, of his resilience.

"Ready for this?" Mia whispered, sneaking up behind him, her presence always a calming influence.

"As ready as I'll ever be. Controlling what I can control," he replied with a grin.

The referee's whistle pierced the air, signaling the start of the match. From the outset, the game was intense. Both teams were evenly matched, creating a nail-biting spectacle.

As the minutes ticked by, Alex felt the weight of the occasion. Every pass, every move he made was met with roaring approval or collective gasps from the crowd. And with every touch of the ball, he was reminded of his journey.

The opposition team, sensing the emotion of the occasion, played with a ferocity that caught Alex's team off-guard. By halftime, they were two goals down.

In the locker room, the atmosphere was tense. The dream of winning the championship, especially for Alex's final game, seemed to be slipping away.

Alex, usually the motivator, was lost in thought. And then, he remembered the bison, the lessons from the meadow and the battle to recover from his injury. With renewed vigor, he stood up, addressing his teammates.

Lesson 2: Trying to avoid the storm only makes things worse. "Challenges are part of life," he began. "Adversity is guaranteed. We're in it right now. The question is how will we respond? Will we try to avoid this moment, try to ignore the reality of the situation? Will we shrink back in fear? Will we let the Critic within take us out? Or will we stick together and face it? We can't control the circumstances. We're down 2-0. It is what it is. Stress is not about the situation, it is about our response to a situation. We control our response. The only way through it is through it. How we respond to adversity is what separates average leaders and teams from great leaders and teams. I believe we have greatness within us. Listen to the Champion inside of you. Let's go into the storm, together. Let's have a bison mentality. Let's not just go into the storm, let's become the storm. Force them to respond. Let's go get this win."

His words, heartfelt and genuine, resonated with the team. They remembered their collective journey, the highs and lows, the victories, and defeats.

As the second half commenced, the team played with renewed energy and determination. They pressed forward, and within minutes, scored their first goal. The stadium erupted, the momentum was shifting..

Off the field, Mia rallied the supporters. Their chants of support filled the air.

Lesson 3: There is power in the herd. Just as Alex had relied on his 'herd' during challenging times, today, the collective strength of the team and supporters was evident. Every pass, every shot, was cheered, every defensive move celebrated. The crowd played as crucial a role as the players on the field. Meanwhile, the crowd for the other team, filled with concern, had gotten quiet. The opponent mirrored their anxiousness.

With minutes left on the clock and the score level, Alex found himself with the ball at his feet, facing the opponent's goal. Time seemed to slow. He remembered his father's words, the lessons learned, the strength built. Taking a deep breath, he took the shot.

The ball soared, curving perfectly, and nestled into the net past the goalkeeper's diving hands. The stadium erupted in a deafening roar. They had taken the lead.

The final whistle blew minutes later, sealing the victory. The team rushed to Alex, lifting him on their shoulders, celebrating not just the win but the end of an era.

As the celebrations continued on the field, Alex caught Mia and his family in the stands. Their journey, filled with storms and rainbows, had led to this moment. Just then Sam rushed over, brimming with excitement. "We did it! Champs!"

Lesson 4: Every storm runs out of rain. This game, much like their journey, had its challenges. But they weathered the storm, emerging stronger, together. The struggle they felt in the first half was replaced with the joy of victory. Had they given up, had they run away from the storm, they would've been walking off the field filled with frustration and regret.

After the medal ceremony, as the crowd started to disperse, Alex addressed the fans. With emotion choking his voice, he thanked them for their unwavering support. "This victory," he began, "isn't just mine, or the team's. It's ours. Each one of you played a part, and for that, I'm beyond grateful."

But he had one final message, especially for the younger generation looking up to him. "In life, as in sport, always remember there will be challenges. It's not about the challenges, it's about how you respond to them. The obstacles can overwhelm you or you can learn to overcome them. Adversity is guaranteed. What we do with it is up to us. Champions in sports, and in life, become champions because they refuse to back down when faced with adversity."

Lesson 5: Do hard things. As he left the field, amidst a sea of applause, this lesson echoed in his mind. His journey, filled with challenges, was testament to the power of resilience, support, and the will to always rise above adversity.

That evening, as celebrations continued, Mia handed Alex a gift. Unwrapping it, he found a framed photograph. It was an image of a bison, standing strong amidst a storm. Below it, inscribed in elegant script, were the words, "Into the storm, bison mentality."

Tears welled up in Alex's eyes. This journey had come full circle. From a young, frustrated player facing adversity to a mentor, advocate, and champion, the storms had shaped him. And as he looked at Mia, he realized that every challenge, every storm, was worth it, for it had led him to this moment, surrounded by love, gratitude, and the promise of new beginnings.

EPILOGUE: EMBRACING THE STORM

The sun was rising over the horizon one morning, the skies beginning to awaken. Alex stood at the edge of the meadow with a cup of coffee, the same place where his father had once told him the tale of the bison and the cow. Time had a way of coming full circle, and today, standing beside Alex, was his own son, Max, eagerly waiting to hear a story.

"You know, Max," Alex began, his voice gentle, filled with nostalgia, "Your grandfather once told me a tale here, a tale that shaped my life in ways I could have never imagined."

And so, while taking in a slow morning with his son, Alex narrated the story of the bison and the cow. He spoke of adversity, of storms, and of the lessons he'd learned along the way.

Max listened intently, absorbing every word, every emotion. He questioned, he wondered, and he empathized.

Through the story, he traveled the journey of his father's life— the highs, the lows, the triumphs, and the tribulations.

As the meadow radiated in the sunlight, the warmth of the sunrise surrounded father and son. Max, considering the stories and lessons, finally said, "Dad, I promise, I'll always remember the bison. I'll face my storms, learn from them, and grow with them. The bison mentality is what we do."

Alex hugged Max, holding him close as he remembered his journey.

As they walked back, hand in hand, the journey of 'Into the Storm' came to a poignant end. But in many ways, it was a new beginning. For in sharing his story, in passing down the wisdom of generations, Alex, much like his father and grandfather before him, had ensured that the legacy of the bison would continue, guiding, inspiring, and illuminating the path for many more generations to come.

Because in the end, life's beauty isn't in avoiding the storms but in learning to embrace them, overcome them, and emerging stronger on the other side.

A massive thank you goes out to those who have supported this project, but especially the launch team. They've given feedback, shared the message with their network and been an incredible support system. They are rock stars.

Kelly Bommer

Tom Buchheim

Dena Scott

Jennifer Chandler

Zach McGinty

Justin Newell

Becky Barker

Rick Bough

Jared Cecil

Terry Saul

Matt King

James Tatum

Alex Perna

Tina McCorkle

Steve Wilson

Chris Meek

Mike Snyder

Derrick Bussman

Jeremy Edwards

Sean Miller

Michael Madrid

Alan Lollar

Dan Christ

Greg Bamberger

Maco Balkovec

Monica Evans

Jerome Learman

Mark Gress, Jr

Ryan Holmes

Dan Rohde

Alyson Wolfe

Jay Fletcher

John Hulen

James Rice

Jake Meyer

Lynn DeBolt Schroeder

Andy Stark

MG Bailey

JP Abercrumbie

Brad Heethuis

Justin Flake

Robert Cortez

Nick Moen

Amy Newberry

Matt Day

Keith Riggs

Renee Carroll

Patti McGowan

Kaycee Tripp

Coby Mackin

Owen Field

ABOUT THE AUTHOR

As the Co-Founder of BETTER and a partner at global leadership development firm GiANT, Kevin DeShazo works with some of the best leaders, teams and organizations in the industry of sports on mindset, leadership and performance.

A sought after keynote speaker, he has presented on more than 400 college campuses, dozens of Fortune 100 companies, and headlined top conferences and conventions.

He has appeared in Sports Illustrated, ESPN.com, The New York Times, Bleacher Report, USA Today and a number of other national and local media platforms. He has written three previous books, *iAthlete: impacting student-athletes of a digital generation* and the Amazon best-sellers *Leadership Interrupted: daily inspiration to become the leader you were meant to be* and *Keep Chopping Wood: an ordinary approach to achieving extraordinary success.*

He calls Oklahoma City home, along with his wife, Megan, and their three boys, Gabe, Noah and Asher.

To book Kevin for your event, email kevin@deshazo.me, call 405.535.6943 or visit his website at www.deshazo.me. If you are a leader in the sports world, you can partner with BETTER at bebetterleaders.com.

If you are a coach or athletic director you can get The Culture Playbook, the signature program from BETTER, at bebetterleaders.com/the-culture-playbook.

If you want to take the concepts from this book to the next level, Kevin has created a resource called 30 Days to a Bison Mentality, with 30 days of exercises and reflections, backed by science, to build your mental toughness. Get that at https://kevindeshazo.gumroad.com/l/bison-mentality.

NOTES

NOTES

NOTES

NOTES

NOTES

NOTES

NOTES

NOTES

NOTES

NOTES

NOTES

NOTES

Made in the USA
Monee, IL
28 December 2024

75565320R00049